MW00438368

Paradise At Its Best

Jackie Herbert

Copyright © 2016 Jackie Herbert

All rights reserved.

ISBN-13: 978-1523717002

Photography by Jackie Herbert

CONTENTS

Dedication

Acknowledgments

Introduction

DEDICATION

Live your dreams to the fullest! Today, I write this book, "Paradise At Its Best," and dedicate this book to my husband, Clifton L. Herbert, for making it all possible! My husband and I have been together for 25 years, and in 2015, we celebrated our 15th Wedding Anniversary. In all the years we have been together, my husband and I enjoyed many vacations, most of which were planned spur of the moment, where we visited many cities throughout Florida. When I wasn't vacationing with my husband, in Florida, I was an Internal Auditor, during my career, where I traveled through various cities within the state.

Seven years ago, on New Year's Eve, December 31, 2008, Cliff and I relocated to Land O' Lakes, Florida, from Abingdon, Maryland! We moved almost

1000 miles from Maryland, which we both resided all of our life. We chose Florida, because you don't pay state income tax. We knew with Cliff's pension we would be able to afford to make this move. The two of us traveled to Florida for vacations and business, for more then 19 years. We grew to like the outdoor life, warm weather, white sandy beaches, nature and wildlife and knew some day this would be our permanent destination.

After, a year of getting acclimated to our new life, in the sunshine state, we both became bored. We decided to open a business which included Handyman, Landscaping and Customized Cleaning. We each dedicate about 5 to 7 hours a day, no weekends and enjoy our down time, with our dog, Nina and guests who come visit. Our hobbies are biking, hiking and photography.

Thank you Cliff, for making this possible for us to live the American Dream, on the west coast of Florida!Life doesn't get any better then this! I love you to the moon and back....xoxo

ACKNOWLEDGMENTS

After relocating to Land O' Lakes, Florida seven years ago, I took a hobby, of taking over ten thousand pictures, of my every day life in Florida. A friend of mine, Denise Moreau Ward, whom I hadn't seen in thirty six years, convinced me I should write a book and share my life in paradise, with the world. I have been sharing my journey, of my relocation through photography, on Facebook, with all my friends and family, where some have chose to take this same journey.

Thank you Sharon Larkin, for all your help in our transition to Land O' Lakes, Florida on New Year's Eve, December, 31, 2008. Your help, once we arrived at our final destination was very much appreciated. There are so many things to know that my book will tell you what

to expect during the transition to Florida.

INTRODUCTION

Looking to relocate from one state to another is a big decision. It must be the right time in your life, you should be financially stable and be able to accept change. You need to prepare yourself for some bumps in the road and take it all in stride. After making a move from one state to another, moving a thousand miles away, leaving all your family and friends behind, I have learned to make a new life for me and my husband, and still stay connected to everyone, through social networks such as Facebook and Skype. One of my biggest hobbies is photography. Over the past seven years, my camera is with me everywhere I go, so I continuously share pictures of everything we do, from dining, to beaches, outdoor activities, sunrises, sunsets, wildlife and much more. In this book, I will be sharing with you the road to relocation, from another state to central Florida, on the west coast. This was a very big decision we made and there is lots to know when preparing for this transition. Hopefully, with the information I share, this will help you to make the right choices when making your decision.

CHAPTER 1

PREPARATION FOR TRANSITION

Throughout our lives, I think we all are thinking where we should be living, whether it be in our early adult life or senior adult life. We question ourselves every day, and with all the social networking available to us, we get to see how others are living their lives.

I have been vacationing in Florida since I was seventeen years old. It started when I went on vacation with a high school friend. Her parents took us to Myrtle Beach, SC, when they became dissatisfied with our hotel arrangements, they decided we were not going to stay and we would be taking our vacation to Daytona Beach, Florida, where they had relatives. I was so excited, I always heard good things about a vacation in Florida, but never thought I would see the day that I would make it there.

This was a beginning with no end to me, I have since vacationed and worked in Florida for the next 30 years of my life. I traveled from the east to the west coast, in the following cities, St. Augustine, Daytona Beach, Ormond Beach, Jacksonville, Orlando, Kissimmee, Melbourne, Vero Beach, West Palm, Stuart, Naples, Key Largo and Key West. You would think after visiting all these cities, by now I have my mind made up to move to the state of Florida. Hold on, not quite yet. It definitely has to be the right time in your life. My husband was a Federal Firefighter, through his career, and after he put his 35 years of service, he would then be able to retire. With my husband being married previously, his children were young, it would not be a good decision, to take away his visitation and the ability to watch them grow. As for me, I worked in the stock brokerage industry for 32 years, started as a clerk and climbed the corporate ladder over the years, with one thing in mind, some day we would embark upon this journey and know that we will be financially stable and it will be the right time to make this transition. Finally, the day would come, in December of 2008.

You could never be too prepared for this

transition we were about to make. It was to

be the most exciting day of my life, but at the

same time we were taking a risk.

My husband being someone who does not

adapt to change, and me being the aggressive

one of the two of us, you would think by now,

he knows through all the years we have been

together, I would not make a big decision like

this and take and run with it, if I didn't think

we could make it work. Yes, we were

nervous, just knowing that you will be leaving

your family and friends behind, not knowing

the next time you will see them, hoping they

will come see us for vacation. All this stuff is

running through your head. Yes, it is true this all plays out in your mind. You need to stay positive, make a checklist of everything you need to do on both ends. Your list from where you will be moving from, should include the following:

List	Phone #	Completion
Movers Company		
Bills to be Paid		
Call Public Utilities, Gas & Elec. and Phone to give disconnect dates		
Call each Creditor give them new address		
Mail Forwarded Magazines Redirected		

Before getting to your destination, be sure to understand you must be able to prove residency. You will need to provide the following information in order to get your Public Utilities/Water account established.

1. Billing name on the account

2. Service Address

3. Date you want service to begin

   - Contact Phone Number

   - A copy of your signed and dated lease if you are renting

   - Proof of Ownership if you are an owner

   - A copy of your current driver's license or State-issued photo ID

- Be prepared to pay a deposit

It is important to find out the name of your power company, that services the area where you will be taking residency. Call them in advance, most companies require a credit check, and they will require the same information needed for Electric Utilities listed above. In addition, some companies require new residents to pay a deposit equal to two times the highest bill or $300.00 (whichever is greater). Other factors may be used in determining deposit requirements. Don't get frustrated about paying a deposit, these large deposits are returned to you within a period of time designated by each company, with interest accruing.

All this information I am sharing with you will help you with your total cost involved in your move. Where exactly in Florida should you move? Paradise in the sunshine state, is absolutely beautiful. Luckily for me, I had experienced some travel through the state to help me make a decision. Some people don't have too many choices, if their job is transferring. Others are looking to start a new chapter in their life, may be able to pick and choose. Each city is unique in its own way. It is important to take a look at the demographics in each area, some areas are Senior Living, Young Retirees, some are working class, and some are young families. Each city from north to south to east to west, they all have different climates. There are areas that have more activities available then others. All of which should be taken into consideration. I will be sharing with you information on living in Paradise and some of my favorite places. Hope this will give you guidance to make the right decision, on whatever path you shall choose to take.

CHAPTER 2

SEASONS

Most people think that Florida doesn't have four seasons. We absolutely do have four seasons. Our state is considered sub-tropical. We don't start to see winter temperatures until January and February. Our winters at times are mild. It all depends on the the jet stream of cold air, that pushes down from the north is when our temperatures will dip down to low thirty degrees overnight. Which at that point and time if you have tropical plants or trees you should cover them so they won't be damaged by frost. We have lots of oak trees that surround us, we see the leaves change colors just like up north, then they fall to the ground. By 9:00 a.m., in the morning, temperatures usually rise to 60 degrees, our high temperature for the day usually will reach 70 degrees in the winter. If we have a mild winter, our temperatures have reached up to 80 degrees. You won't find yourself using a lot of heat down here, during our winter months. There are times that it will actually feel colder in the house then outside, so you open your doors and windows to let the fresh air and warmth come inside.

The months March through May, we are generally in a drought, with very little rain. Temperatures average mid 70's to mid 80's.

This is when all tropical plants and trees are in full bloom.

Here are some of our other seasons:

- *Tornado Season* – June thru September and February thru April.

- *Hurricane Season* – June 1st – November 30th

- *Turtle Nesting Season* – March 1st – October 31st

- *Tree planting Season* in Florida (December – February)

- *Snowbird Season* - Northerners start flocking to Florida typically from October/November thru April/May.

- *Spiny Lobster Season* – Regular Season is August 6th through March 31st

- *Manatee Season* - officially October 15th thru March 31st but Manatees stay in some areas all year long.

CHAPTER 3

ACTIVITIES

Living on the west coast, in central Florida, where

your temperatures are primarily mild throughout the year,

there is so much to do outdoors. In this chapter I am

going to share some of my favorite places and the various

activities available to you.

Photography had become one of my biggest hobbies,

for the reason, after moving to Florida, there is so much

wildlife, nature, beautiful sunrises, sunsets and having

some of the most beautiful white sandy beaches you have

ever seen. While sharing with you some of my favorite

and the many activities available, I will display some of

my photography, so you can see it through your own

eyes. You know the saying, "A picture is worth a thousand words."

I think when most people move to Florida, young children, young adults and our seniors, many invest in some type of bike. Biking is one of the best cardio exercises for people of all ages, mainly because Florida primarily is a flat state. It gets you out into the sunshine to absorb some vitamin D, keeps you active and every time you ride, you will see some of the most beautiful nature and wildlife surround you, where every day the scenery is different. When you choose your route to bike you can limit yourself to a short ride through the neighborhood or choose to go to one of the many bike trails, parks or preserves to take longer rides.

One of my favorite trails is the Suncoast Trail, it is a 42 mile paved trail that stretches through three counties,

Hillsborough, Pasco and Hernando. You can ride your bike until your heart is content. The trail is open from dawn to dusk and has many entrances throughout these three counties, some of which include some amenities, such as a port-o-let, restroom, public telephone, water supply or cooler and four information kiosks. This trail does not limit someone to bike use, you will find many joggers, people roller blading or power walking.

The Fred Marquis Pinellas Trail is another which extends from St. Petersburg to Tarpon Springs, the trail is 38 miles and is also a multi-use trail for you to bike, jog, walk or skate. This trail passes through the towns of Dunedin, Clearwater, Largo, Seminole, South Pasadena and Gulfport. Some people choose to use this trail for their commute back and forth to work. While on the trail you will travel through coastal communities, parks, water areas and natural settings.

There are reports that there are over 70,000 people ride this trail on a monthly basis. Beautiful trail to enjoy taking the family or friends and see lots of wildlife along the way.

There are many other cycling trails throughout the Tampa Bay Area. You will also see there are lots of water sport activities at the Beaches, on the Rivers and the Bayous.

CHAPTER 4

ENTERTAINMENT

There is so much entertainment for everyone. Something to do almost every day. In this chapter, I will share with you some of the exciting entertainment that I recommend to see.

Gasparilla is when the Swashbucklers, revelry and the hunt for the hidden treasure. The seasonal celebration pays respect to Tampa's last great mythical buccaneer, Jose Gaspar, who was known for terrorizing West Florida's coastal waters during the 18th early 19th century. When Gaspar died, folklore tells of the buried fortune, that they claim still is undiscovered, somewhere along the west coast. The invasion continues every year, but they expanded to three months, from the end of January til March, which includes parades, parties, art, film, music and much more.

Florida State Fair has been going on annually, for over 110 years and it welcomes visitors for two weeks. You can explore the agriculture exhibits with thousands of animals and you will find over 100 rides on one of the largest midways in the U.S. There will be a lot of traditional fair foods or the latest concoctions, for the visitors to sample.

Strawberry Festival is an annual event that last for about 11 days and generates an attendance of about half a million patrons from all over Central Florida and beyond. The festival is a venue for flea market style craft and item sales, various free entertainment, very large midway, plus big name musical concert performances and livestock activities.

Florida Botanical Gardens, which is located in Largo, Florida, with over 30 acres of cultivated gardens and 90 acres of natural areas. Free admission daily to visitors.

Botanical Gardens

Crystal River is known as, The Home of the Manatee and is located in Crystal River, Florida. There is so much

to see and do, which includes fishing, birdwatching, camping, boating, snorkeling, kayaking and swimming, with the manatees. There is Mullet Key, which is historical island near Crystal River. Three Sisters Springs is where you can canoe, kayak and swim, with the manatees, where water temperature stays about 72 degrees year round. You also have the Crystal River Archaeological State Park, which is a 61 acre historical landmark pre-Columbian, Native American site.

Manatee Viewing Center is located at the Big Bend Power Station in Apollo Beach. When Tampa Bay reaches a temperature of 68 degrees or colder, large numbers of manatees swim into the power station discharge canal. You will find the education building teaches you about the manatees and their habitat. On the outside of the center you will see some butterfly gardens and some Florida friendly landscaping. As you stroll along the walk you will encounter some other wildlife that has made this their habitat. It is free admission to visitors. It is open from November 1 – April 15.

Weeki Wachee River – located in Hernando County, 7 miles long, where you can enjoy all the nature coast has to offer. You will experience crystal clear waters, with a slow moving current downstream, while canoeing, kayaking, board paddling or swimming, in quaint little coves along the way, with your family and friends. Temperature of the water stays 72 degrees year round. You can either use your own canoes, kayaks or boards for a small nominal fee or you will find several local vendors who make them available for rent. While floating down the river you will encounter some manatees, dolphins, otters, aquatic birds and much more.

WeekiWachee River

Ybor City, one of Florida's top ranked nightspots

located in a historic neighborhood in Tampa, Florida, just northeast of downtown. It is known as Tampa's Latin Quarter. You will find different types of cuisine like Spanish, Cuban, Italian, Greek and French. You can browse the many shops, museums and stay for the night time entertainment including jazz, blues, salsa, reggae and even hip-hop.

Bush Gardens located in Tampa, it is a family adventure park, which includes wild rides, wildlife encounters, live entertainment and more.

Riverwalk located in downtown Tampa, Florida. Family fun includes dining, shopping, hotels, playgrounds and more. Here is some of what you will see while on the Riverwalk.

- ➢ The Florida Aquarium which has over 20,000 Aquatic Plants and Animals from all over the world.

- ➢ Channelside Bay Plaza, where you will find shops, dining, bowling and entertainment.

- ➢ Tampa Bay History Center, where you will see exhibits from Native Inhabitants from around the Tampa Bay Area.

- ➢ Curtis Hixon Waterfront Park, which is the centerpiece of the Riverwalk. Park has two splash-zones, children's playground, public boat docks, vendors and a dog park.

Ruth Eckerd Hall is a performing arts venue, located in

Clearwater, in the Tampa Bay Area! Throughout the year there are many performances ranging from world renowned classical artists and dance companies to Broadway musicals and pop stars.

Straz Center

Straz Center is a Performing Arts Venue, located in Tampa along the Hillsborough River, home to five halls, three restaurants, a coffee shop and the Patel

Conservatory.

Tampa's Lowery Park Zoo, is a 63 acre, non profit zoo located in Tampa, Florida. In 2009, it was voted the #1 Zoo by Parent Magazine because how close children can get to interact with the animals. You will find over 1000 animals, with many exhibits. The park has concession and picnic areas for the visitors.

Tarpon Springs, known as the Sponge Capital of the World and is located along the Gulf of Mexico. Some of the attractions are the Natural Sponges, Dolphins, Sunset Cruises, Diving, Shopping Greek Restaurants, bakeries and live entertainment.

Tarpon Springs

Walt Disney World, located in Orlando, Florida has (4)
Theme Parks, they are Magic Kingdom, Epcot,
Hollywood Studios, and Animal Kingdom.

There are two Water Parks, Disney's Typhoon Lagoon
and Disney's Blizzard Beach.

Professional Baseball Spring Training is held during the months of February and March. The state of Florida has been hosting some of the teams for over 100 years. Included here you will find the 15 teams and their locations.

- > **Atlanta Braves** – ESPN Wide World of Sports.

  Walt Disney World Resort,

  Kissimmee, FL 34747

- > **Baltimore Orioles** – Ed Smith Stadium,

  2700 12th Street

  Sarasota, FL 34237

- > **Boston Redsox**- Jet Blue Park,

  11500 Fenway South Drive,

  Fort Myers, FL 33913

➢ **Detroit Tigers** – Joker Marchant Stadium,

    2125 North Lake Avenue,

    Lakeland, FL 33805

➢ **Houston Astros**- Osceola County Stadium,

    631 Heritage Parkway,

    Kissimmee, FL 34744

➢ **Miami Marlins** – Roger Dean Stadium,

    4751 Main Street,

    Jupiter, FL 33458

➢ **Minnesota Twins** – Hammond Stadium at
Century Link Sports Complex

    14100 Six Mile Cypress Pkwy,

    Fort Myers, FL 33912

- ➤ **New York Mets** – Tradition Field,

  525 NW Peacock Blvd.,

  Port St. Lucie, FL 34986

- ➤ **New York Yankees** – George M. Steinbrenner Field,

  One Steinbrenner Dr.

  Tampa, FL 33614

- ➤ **Phillies** -Bright House Field,

  601 N. Old Coachman Road,

  Clearwater, FL 33765

- ➤ **Pittsburgh Pirates** – McKechnie Field,

  1611 Ninth Street West,

  Bradenton, FL 34205

- **St. Louis Cardinals** – Roger Dean Stadium,

  4751 Main Street,

  Jupiter, FL 33458

- **Tampa Bay Rays** – Charlotte Sports Park,

  2300 El Jobean Road,

  Port Charlotte, FL 33948

- **Toronto Blue Jays** – Florida Auto Exchange Stadium,

  373 Douglas Avenue,

  Dunedin, FL 34698

- **Washington Nationals** Space Coast Stadium,

  5800 Stadium Pkwy,

  Viera, FL 32940

CHAPTER 5

BEACHES

The sunshine state has a beautiful white sandy beach for everyone! There are many to choose from right off the Gulf of Mexico. Most of them have lots of water sports, fishing, shelling, volleyball, restaurants, cruises and more. Here are some to give you an idea of what the Gulf Coast has to offer.

Fort De Soto Park is the largest park in Pinellas County, it has 1,136 acres made up of five interconnected islands or keys: Madelaine Key, St. Jean Key, St. Christopher Key, Bonne Fortune Key and the main island of Mullet Key. It has two fishing piers, which both have food and bait concession stands. Enjoy over seven miles of waterfront, which includes almost three miles of

Fort DeSoto Park

beautiful white sandy beach where you can rent a canoe or kayak or even take your own boats and catch some of the most beautiful sunsets. If you love the outdoors, they have a 238-site family camping area with facilities. You will encounter some of the most beautiful birds and see lots of dolphins swimming out in the gulf. Don't forget to take some time to check out more then 400 years of history at Fort DeSoto.

Hudson Beach

Hudson Beach is a small quaint, relaxing beach to getaway with the family to soak up some sun. It has an artificial canal, with 25 miles of inland waters. Small peaceful beach to avoid crowds of people. There are few restaurants to grab a nice lunch or dinner or pavilions available to catch the beautiful sunsets at no cost. While strolling down the beach you will see lots of birds and few dolphins swimming out in the gulf.

Clearwater Beach is notoriously ranked one of the best beaches in Florida. The white sandy beach on a 3 mile stretch, of the Pinellas Peninsula, on the Gulf of Mexico. Enjoy sunbathing, beach volleyball, rent fishing boats, para-sailing or even taking a cruise to see the dolphins.

Honeymoon Island, is located off the Gulf of Mexico, in Dunedin, Florida. Visitors drive across Dunedin Causeway to enjoy the white sandy beach, mangrove swamps, and nature trails. Nature lovers will find osprey nests and a wide variety of shorebirds. In the park you will find several nature trails and bird observation areas. While on the Island some of the birds you will observe are, Osprey, Snowy Egrets, great Blue Herons and many other species. You will even see manatees and dolphins swimming out in the gulf. Visitors can swim, fish, and snorkel, in the warm waters of the Gulf or picnic while they enjoy the beautiful scenery. Honeymoon Island is one of the more popular beaches for shelling. The gulf currents deposit a variety of seashells along the shoreline. There are two snack bars on the beach and a gift shop. The facilities offer beach chair, umbrella, bicycles and kayak rentals for a nominal fee.

Caladesi Island State Park is accessible by either a private boat or a by the Caladesi Connection Ferry Service. The cost for the ferry is $14.00 for adults and $7.00 for children ages 6-12. Prices are subject to change. The ferry departs daily starting at 10:00 a.m. from Honeymoon Island. Passengers are allotted a four hour stay on the island. No pets are allowed on the ferry. For additional information you can contact the ferry office on 727-734-1501. The island has tables and grills and you can hike on a beautiful nature trail.

Madeira Beach and John's Pass Village & Boardwalk is a popular attraction in St.Pete/Clearwater. It is known for its waterfront hub for shopping, dining and entertainment. Madeira Beach is a 2.5 mile beach attracts those who are a fan of sun and sea and you will see a lot of fishing, where John's Pass includes over 100 stores and restaurants on the waterfront and offers some deep sea fishing, dolphin cruises and has wave runners available for rental.

Pine Island is in Hernando County, off the Gulf of Mexico. It is also known as, Alfred McKethan Park.

Local vendors are on site to rent a variety of kayaks,

Pine Island

Pine Island

canoes and stand up paddle boards. The Island offers

cool beverages and light fare on site and they also have

picnic tables and small grills to hold a family cookout. If

you are looking for the perfect place to catch a beautiful

sunset, look no further.

Anna Maria Island is located in Manatee County it offers a seven mile strip of white sandy beaches, Coquina Beach, Manatee Beach Bradenton Beach, Cortez Beach and Anna Maria Beach. The beaches offer water sport rentals, volleyball courts, theme parks and water slides. There are nearby restaurants and shops and boutiques. Or just spend the day soaking up the sun, fishing or enjoy watching the wildlife, turtles, birds, manatees or dolphins! Don't forget to stay and watch a beautiful sunset.

Treasure Island is one of St. Pete's longest and widest beaches. Guest enjoy swimming, shelling, snorkeling, para sailing and the beautiful sunsets. You will find lots of dining (many on the waterfront), shopping and nightlife. Annually every fall there is a sand sculpting competition.

St. Pete Beach is located in Pinellas County, just south of Treasure Island and has been known as an award winning beach. Enjoy soaking up the rays on this white sandy beach and other attractions like The Pier, which is a five story dining and shopping complex. Amenities you will find are three boardwalks that are built over natural sand dunes and sea oats that lead to a white sandy swim area. You will also find the historical Grand Don CeSar resort, which opened in 1928 and now serves as a popular retreat for the rich and the famous today.

Siesta Key is located in Sarasota FL. It is perfect for a romantic getaway. Enjoy strolling on the white sandy beach, shell collecting or renting a catamaran or kayak from one of the concessionaires. The beach side also has picnic areas and playgrounds that can be used during your family vacation. Be sure to enjoy the beautiful sunsets!

CHAPTER 6

NATURE/WILDLIFE

Florida is known for it's tropical trees, plants, rivers, bayous and wildlife. Everywhere you travel, there are beautiful Palm trees, of all sizes and shapes used for landscaping. There are over 2500 different type, just to name a few, you have the Sabal Palm, Pineapple Palm, Royal Palms, Sago Palm, Silver Palm and many more. You will also see many Oak, Cypress and Pine Trees. The Oak and Cypress trees tend to have Spanish Moss that will grow on the tree. Spanish moss is an epiphyle plant that absorbs nutrients and water from the air. The plant has no ariel roots, it propagates by seed that blows in the wind and it will stick to the tree limbs or it sometimes is carried by birds, as a nesting material.

I am most attracted to the beautiful lakes, bayous and rivers that surround me. Florida has more than 30,000 lakes, range from small to large. Alligators are common in lakes, rivers and streams. When one leaves, another will show up. You will usually see a bayou, on the gulf coast, which is known as a marshy outlet of a lake. You will also see lots of rivers where there is a lot of boating, kayaking, canoeing and fishing happening.

Always stay alert when walking around lakes, rivers or streams. Alligators are very common in Florida. They relocate during the summer months, during their mating season. Alligator population continues to grow rapidly. Most gators you will encounter are less then 6 feet and they usually stay away from people. If they should become aggressive, Florida has a Nuisance

Alligator Program, where they will send a licensed

trapper to trap and remove the animal. In most cases this

alligator will then be euthanized.

Gator

Then you have the dolphins, which are usually seen

in the coastal waters. There are various venues where

you can go swim, with the dolphins or you can simply sit

on the shore and watch them swim out in the gulf.

Another marine mammal you will see while out in coastal waters, rivers or bays, is the manatee. The manatee is a large aquatic relative of the elephant. In the winter months, 100's of them will swim into the Power Plant in Apollo Beach or up in Crystal River. They usually are not found in temps below 68 degrees.

We also encounter an abundance of the gopher tortoise all over Florida. They will dig their burrows in dry habitats. The tortoise and their burrows are protected by the state of Florida. They must be relocated before any development can take place on any land. If you are helping a turtle cross the road, you should move them in the direction they were traveling. A tortoise is directional and if you move them the opposite direction, they will still turn around and head back into the road.

As for birds, in Florida, we have 1000's of different type birds live here all year round, you will see in the marsh areas, lakes, and Gulf Coast. Then in the winter months, you have many that will migrate south from the northern states. Some of the most beautiful birds you may encounter are some Egrets, Herons, Hawks, Cranes, Eagles, Pelicans, Woodpeckers, Double Crested Cormorant, ducks and more. The sandhill cranes are a very large bird, silver/gray color with a red patch on their crown. Usually, you see them in pairs because they mate for life. Every year the female will lay two eggs and the juveniles will stay with their parents until they are 9-10 months. These cranes are entertaining, they are known for their dancing skills, stretching their wings and leaping in the air. Usually, when you see a pair, they become very territorial and seem to get very agitated when other sandhill cranes come near them. Especially. during their

mating season.

Sandhill Crane

Sandhill Crane

The American Black Duck you will also see a lot of

them. They are a dusky brown color, both males and

females look alike, but the female is a little lighter in

color. This duck usually breeds during March – May and

will lay 7-17 eggs within 29 days the eggs will hatch.

You will find the mamma and her babies swimming around the lakes, hanging out in the marsh areas and even walking up in your yards.

American Black Duck

One of the most desirable sports most Floridians and tourist, on vacation take an interest in fishing. Central Florida Public Beaches allow fishing from the shore and by boat. Inshore fishing you might catch snook, pompano, snapper and red fish. Some beaches have

fishing piers. Otherwise there are thousands of salt water

fish in Florida. A Florida fishing license is required to

land saltwater species in Florida regardless of where they

are caught (state or federal water). Refer to

myfwc.com/license/recreational/saltwater-fishing/

CHAPTER 7

SUNRISE/SUNSETS

Every day I wake up I can hardly wait to see the sunrise. I am mesmerized every day to see a beautiful sunrise and every one is different. There are a couple vendors who offer Hot Air Balloon rides to capture some of the most beautiful sunrises. As for me, I enjoy watching the Hot Air Balloons fly by, with the beautiful sunrise behind them.

The west coast of central Florida offers many venues or sailing out to sea to see some of the most spectacular sunsets. You can capture some of the most beautiful sunsets right from the shore or you can go to one of the venues that offer cruises, with dinners for a nominal fee.

Hot Air Balloon with Sunrise

Here a few venues that offer sunset cruises:

Odyssey Sunset Cruise - It's a 2 hour sunset cruise down the Anclote River, into the Gulf of Mexico. While on the cruise you will learn about the historical Tarpon

Springs and the famous sponge docks. For additional information please see their website at

http://odysseycruises.net/

Calypso Queen Dinner Cruise – Cruise the Clearwater Harbor, for 2 hours, while enjoying the sunset, with dancing and for additional fees you can enjoy a Tropical Dinner and Open Bar. For additional information, please see their website, http://calypsoqueen.com

Yacht Starship Dining Cruises – Cruising with a 360 degree view of Tampa Bay for 2 ½ hours, which includes, dining and dancing. For additional information, please see their website

http://www.yachtstarship.com

There are so many sunset cruises with or without dining, lots of charters you can either go alone or set up a cruise to sail with a group.

CHAPTER 8

FINAL DESTINATION

There are big decisions to be made with any relocation. Is Central Florida where you want to relocate? Some of the many reasons why people move to Florida, there is no state income tax, the climate varies from subtropical in the north to tropical in the south, lower cost of living, beaches, there are lots of recreational sports, (biking, fishing, water sports, golf etc...) and it's a vacation destination. Many residents are transplants from other states and some of the recent demographics indicate there are close to 1000 people move to Florida each day, which include retirees and many young working class families.

Every day I wake up, I am mesmerized by the beautiful sunrise, sunsets, wildlife and nature. I really believe when the sun shines almost every day of the year, it makes people happy.

Always do your research before making such a big decision before transitioning to another state. I can say that this was one of the best decisions my husband and I made and there is no turning back. We have reached our final destination!

Hope the information and photography I have shared gives you some ideas for either relocating or vacationing.

We are Living the American Dream!

Our Home

Paradise

Made in the USA
Las Vegas, NV
12 May 2021

22933167R00040